Risky Business,
a.k.a., Dawg

R. J. Hammond

Archway Publishing books may be ordered through booksellers or by contacting:

Archway Publishing
1663 Liberty Drive
Bloomington, IN 47403
www.archwaypublishing.com
1 (888) 242-5904

Because of the dynamic nature of the Internet, any web addresses or links contained in this book may have changed since publication and may no longer be valid. The views expressed in this work are solely those of the author and do not necessarily reflect the views of the publisher, and the publisher hereby disclaims any responsibility for them.

Any people depicted in stock imagery provided by Getty Images are models, and such images are being used for illustrative purposes only.
Certain stock imagery © Getty Images.

ISBN: 978-1-4808-9321-4 (sc)
ISBN: 978-1-4808-9322-1 (e)

Library of Congress Control Number: 2020913304

Print information available on the last page.

Archway Publishing rev. date: 8/25/2020

CONTENTS

My favorite mother-in-law loved Risky and if she told me once she told me 25 times that I should write about Risky. We lost Ruby House 2 years ago but she was instrumental in urging me to write a book about that dog. Well, I did it Ruby and thank you very much and I know you are looking down and smiling at my effort.

Risky
2005-2019

ONE

I grew up with dogs, mostly mixed breeds and strays—dogs that, for the most part, would show up at houses and someone would feed them. My family moved from Texarkana, Texas, to Eunice, New Mexico, when I was three years old. Shortly after that my dad got a job with Phillips, and we moved to Oil Center to live in a gas camp that was two miles from the nearest store. There was an El Paso camp about a quarter mile to the west, and we all rode a school bus to Eunice to attend classes.

There were a lot of dogs around, and they seemed

to go to wherever they could get fed and taken care of. - The ones that weren't really pets and didn't belong to anyone always seemed to scrounge up food somewhere. You might have a dog around to feed and play with until they found a better deal. The camps were surrounded by mesquite bushes that tended to have a rattlesnake curled up under them. You could easily go out rabbit hunting and end up shooting a snake or, in my case, dropping the rifle and running away as fast as you could. I was pretty fast anyhow, but rattlers made me faster.

Several dogs got bitten through the years. On one occasion my brother was out hunting with some friends when his dog, Ginger, jumped between a rattler and one of the boys and was bitten. Unfortunately, Ginger didn't survive.

Growing up in a gas camp with dogs around to play with was an experience I am glad I had. Besides rabbits there were quail and dove in abundance, and hunting and eating quail was my favorite thing to do. We used to fry and eat the rabbits we killed out hunting, but after an outbreak of bubonic plague, my dad started raising white rabbits to eat. He had pens for the rabbits, as did other men in the camp, who also raised rabbits or chickens.

If our dog at the time and I crossed the blacktop between the two camps, we could walk the two miles to the store on an oil road. The road had to be oiled to keep the sandstorms from being so bad. The wind blew a lot in eastern New Mexico and west Texas. As a matter of fact, the wind blew so hard at times that we had to throw a blanket over the horse's rear to keep the wind from blowing the bit out of his mouth. I would walk to Crow's Grocery and buy a box of .22-caliber shells and a pack of unfiltered Camels for less than five dollars. The Camels were for my dad, of course.

I would not have called many of the dogs my pets because my mother would not allow dogs in the house. We built doghouses, and that was where they slept. I also don't think the dogs knew what cats were because they were few and far between. So the dogs mostly chased their tails and each other.

When I left home to go out and build a future, I had several dogs. The first was a cocker spaniel named Eric Von Zipper, a name borrowed from the *Beach Blanket Bingo* movies. Next came a shih tzu named Shi Shi, bred to keep your toes warm. He was a cute dog but not too smart. When our son, Jared, was around ten, we decided to get a real dog, so we found a black Lab puppy and took him home. We named him Hobbs because a friend of Jared's had a dog named Calvin. Our daughter, Kasey, then decided she had to have her own dog. We found one for sale in the newspaper and drove all the way across the state to Pueblo to pick up the dog. The kids of the family with the dog walked up to the meeting spot and said they were broken down, so we drove down under I-25 to an underpass where the dog was. The dog looked like he had never had a bath or brushing. But my daughter just had to have him. There was also a monkey in their van; I said, "No, thanks!" to the monkey. We got the dog home and gave him a bath and a good brushing, and he was as good as new. Every time he was in the house and a monkey came on TV, he would cover his eyes up.

Kasey named him Bogota, a town close to where her mom grew up, because Hobbs was close to a town where I grew up. They were strange names maybe, but my brother David once named a dog Number Four.

Risky
2005-2019

TWO

Okay, okay, let's talk about the best dog ever. We met some friends for breakfast before going to a flyball tournament next to Uranium Downs in Grand Junction. Flyball is a dog relay, where four dogs jump on a vertical board and a tennis ball is ejected out; the dog catches it and returns it to the start. We had lost Hobbs to the same thing that put Marley down, and we were not looking for another dog at the tournament. Our friends, however, were interested in a dog, and they were looking at one at the flyball race. We took the dog for a walk at the nearby botanical gardens. We found a place to sit, and I took the dog off the leash. The woman who owned the dog had rescued him but didn't have time to train him to run relay races. His name was Risky Business. He wandered around a bit while we visited, and when we got ready to go back and watch flyball, I called for him. Risky came around the corner and headed toward me. When he reached me, he promptly laid his head in my lap. I looked at Tonya, my wife, for approval and said, "We're taking this dog home."

We took the Risky home, and Valynn brought her standard poodle to play with Risky. They ran and played, chased each other, and even barked and growled, trying to put the other in their place. It didn't take long to figure out why the woman was getting rid of Risky—when he fetched a ball or a dog toy, it was his, and you weren't getting it. No one could catch him. I was amazed by how fast he was. I sent a picture of Risky to both my kids and immediately got a response from our daughter, Kasey. She wrote, "Dad, that is the ugliest dog I have ever seen." A couple of weeks later, Kasey came home for the weekend and quickly changed her mind about Risky.

Risky was a strange-looking dog for sure. He was a

mix between a greyhound, deerhound, and border collie, and we quickly learned not only how fast he was but how smart he was. Later on I told my kids he was smarter than both of them put together. Risky certainly minded me better than they ever did.

Risky and I started to feel each other out. I was not certain of what we had in this dog, and he was already determining how to manipulate me. We started walking every day, first in the neighborhood and then at Canyon View Park, a park of around five acres, where there was plenty of room for him to run. At the park there were several ponds around, with lots of ducks swimming and geese flying overhead. I would let Risky off the leash, and he would run, trying his best to catch a goose. He would also venture out into one of the ponds to try to catch a duck, but they would just quack at him because he refused to swim after them. One day he did go out too far. His feet lost the bottom, and he quickly swam the two feet to reach the pond's bottom. I never saw him attempt to swim again.

We discovered a dog park across the street and started going there. I never saw any dog that could catch Risky. He soon got tired of the dog park, and we went back to the big park. Risky started getting me into trouble because I was letting him chase anything and everything. The dog catcher got us one day and informed us that a leash was mandatory. After that we just went out earlier, while the dog catcher was still sleeping. Risky liked to run but also did a lot of stopping and sniffing. He was usually behind me, and when he took off, he would take a wide berth around me at full speed. I was always a little uneasy about that—and for good reason. Sometimes we would take Bogota to the park with us, and Risky loved that because he would run at full speed, knock Bogota over, and send him tumbling along the ground. There were usually guys at the park flying airplanes, drones, or kites, and it just fascinated Risky, as he tried to catch them. A couple of guys would even buzz him, but that just made him more determined. One time I thought Risky was going to attack one of the low-flying planes, but the guy yelled at him, so he backed off.

There were always soccer or baseball games going on at one or more of the fields. A little league team was practicing there one day, and we were crossing behind them when a ball came flying out over the head of the outfielder. Risky knocked the kid down trying to get the ball. Thank goodness the boy was okay, but Risky got a good scolding.

One morning we were at the park fairly early, avoiding the dog catcher. While going around the ponds, Risky was ahead of me and kept hiding behind trees that weren't very big. He kept moving from tree to tree, thinking I couldn't see him. A few minutes later he was behind me and I was walking backward, watching him. He was about thirty feet behind me when he started running straight at me. I stepped to the left, and he went to the right and hit my knee, knocking me down. He came and lay down beside me and put his head on my chest, as if to say, "My bad." I called my wife and told her I had fallen and couldn't get up. She came to the park and picked us up. She got me home and settled, but after about thirty minutes I told her that I thought my leg was broken. She called me a pansy but took me to the ER anyway. The x-ray came back with a vertical break just below the knee. A couple of people actually asked me if I put Risky down.

Risky
2005-2019

THREE

Risky spent a lot of time hiding from me, trying to trick me, and generally, just being a dog. A little after we got Risky, we started going to the desert for our walks, where there was no dog catcher. There was a lot of gullies out there that were about fifty feet deep and one hundred feet across, with forks about every quarter of a mile. Risky loved it in the desert because there were a lot of rabbits to chase. He was always ahead of me, and when he came to a fork, he chose one and kept going, but when I finally got there, he was standing at the next turn and looking back for me. He would at times just run up the sides of the gullies, looking for something to chase. Sometimes I wouldn't see him for ten or fifteen minutes, but all of a sudden he would come back down ahead of me. No matter which way I went, he knew exactly where I was.

One day when we were out avoiding the gullies, he took off like a shot, running straight at a coyote. I yelled and said, "Watch it; he will break your leg." Risky did find a smaller coyote about his size, and they would take turns chasing each other.

On the east side of the road was a lot of bushes, where rabbits and prairie dogs could hide. A normal prairie dog hole wasn't very big, but after Risky got finished sending dirt flying ten feet in the air, the entrance to the hole was a lot more accessible. I was always concerned he might get stuck in one of those holes.

Sometimes there were cows and calves close to where we walked. One day I suddenly saw Risky take off after one of the calves, and I started yelling and telling him, "No!" The rancher happened to witness Risky's chase and came over and pointed his finger at Risky. He said, "You are fast but you better not chase another calf of mine." As he walked away, I told Risky no more cow chasing and to stop getting me into trouble.

Risky loved the desert because he loved to run so much, and sometimes he would come back from chasing something with his tongue hanging out, looking for the water bowl. There were usually a lot of people out there with their dogs, and he made friends with most of them. A guy I knew would bring his sheep and sheep dog quite a bit, and at times it was a chore to keep Risky away from them.

One afternoon on the way back from the desert, we went over to Valynn's house. All of the dogs could run and play. She also had a cat, and though it was a house cat, it slipped out the door; Risky grabbed it and started to shake it, but thank goodness the cat got away and climbed a tree. After Valynn got the cat back in the house and settled down, she came outside and shook her finger at Risky. I asked her if he could have a treat, and she said, "He tried to eat my cat, and you want me to give him a treat?" I looked at Risky and said, "Cat tastes like chicken."

Another place I took Risky to was much closer to the house and mostly flat, with a few hills around. He would get excited when I turned down the road because he knew exactly where we were headed. He would start panting, and as soon as I opened his door, he was off like he was shot out of a cannon. One day I had just barely got out of the car when he jumped out the front door and took off. I glanced at my watch and started timing him. He reached his destination, a prairie dog hole, in about thirteen seconds. He had run 185 yards—wow!

While Risky was digging, I would walk around the hills to get my exercise, and if he wasn't with me, he was digging for prairie dogs. In order to locate him, I just looked for dirt flying in the air. Late one afternoon we were out there, and the ladies track team from Mesa State College were out running and training for track season. Sometimes we had to stop when they went past us, and one time one of the ladies said, "Hi, cutie."

I said, "Why, thank you."

She replied, "I was talking to the dog." It ruined my afternoon for sure. Risky always got a lot of attention from those ladies.

At times we would go further out toward the Bookcliffs, a mountain range. There was always something for Risky to chase or a place for him to dig.

It amazed me the distance and speed he would go when chasing rabbits. I think he would have caught more rabbits if they would have run in a straight line.

One day I saw him with something in his mouth, and he was shaking the daylights out of it. As I walked up, he dropped a rabbit on the ground. I looked around, and the rabbit hole was only a few feet away. I noticed a big circle in the dirt with a line through it, and on further inspection, I saw a little pair of crutches and some eyeglasses with coke-bottle lenses. I looked at Risky and said, "Sorry, buddy, but not going to let you count this one. Now you are 0 for 279 in your effort to catch a rabbit, and furthermore, you ain't nothing but a hound dog—but I still love you!"

Risky
2005-2019

FOUR

Risky loved to try and trick me. He had a peanut butter bone for eating his dog food in the evening. Risky actually lay down in front of his bowl to eat, and it took him five minutes to finish his dinner. I could always hear him in the next room, chomping and moving food around. One night I was playing games on my phone when he came to me, wanting his treat. I gave him the treat, expecting him to take it outside in the front yard. About a half hour later, I went in the kitchen to get a glass of water and noticed that his bowl still contained dog food. For a few days he tried to trick me again, but I could hear him pushing the food around with his nose, trying to make me think he was eating it. He was a sneaky pup for sure.

Risky seldom went outside at night after we had gone to bed, and if he did, it was usually because he heard a cat out on the fence. He would chase the cat for a bit and then go to the door to be let in. One night he got me up to let him out, and when we got to the door and I opened it for him, he turned and headed to the bedroom. I closed the door and followed him, but when I got there, he was up in the bed in my spot. I told him to move, but he just looked at me and then closed his eyes. That wasn't the last time he pulled that on me.

Risky was pretty good about not doing his business in the grass. There was a large juniper tree in the north end of the yard that was covered in gravel, and Risky would poop under that tree. Our kids lived in Denver, and we made several trips during the year and were usually gone two or three nights. Ann Marie, the woman next door, always took care of Risky when we were gone. We also had a time share in Mesquite, Nevada, and we went several times a year for golf and a little gambling. When we would return from those trips, Risky was so glad to see us. Other times, if we were gone for more than three nights, Risky would whine and pout when we returned home because we were gone too long. After one of those trips, he left me a nice little present out in the backyard.

We took Risky on a few of our trips to Denver, where we always stayed with our daughter. She lived in an apartment complex in Westminster. There were lots of trees there, which also meant there were squirrels and rabbits. Every walk we went on, Risky was looking up for a squirrel or rabbit. Across the street were a lot of townhomes, and all of them had gutters with drainpipes reaching the ground and extending out a few feet. Risky would see a rabbit run in a drainpipe, and he would stick his nose in, trying to get the rabbit. If that didn't work, he would go to the place he thought the rabbit was and put his mouth around the downspout—pretty silly dog if you ask me.

Jared, our son, lived a couple of blocks from Denver University, so Risky and I would take our morning and evening walks there. One time Risky saw a squirrel run up a tree and headed that way. It was a huge tree about three feet off the ground, and where the branches spread, there was a pretty wide spot. Risky jumped up in the crook of the tree and stood up on the branch, trying to reach the squirrel. I was laughing so hard that I had to sit down. I told Risky to get out of the tree. Reluctantly he jumped down and came to me, looking me straight in the eye. I told him if he started acting like a cat, I was going to disown him. Nothing that dog did ever surprised me.

Risky
2005-2019

FIVE

Risky and I walked a lot in Paradise Hills, the subdivision we lived in. We went through the neighborhood a lot, the canal bank just east of our house. We could go one of two ways when we started our walks: head west through part of the neighborhood and wind around to the vacant land to the north or head up the canal bank and south, back toward home. I let him have his head most of the time, so there were many different ways we could go according to his mood. I named the many walks: the long way, the short way, the long short way, the long

long way, the short long way, the really long way, and the really short way, which he refused to go on.

Most people knew Risky's name, and we ran into them a lot on our walks, from the kids at the playground to most others that came down our street. Two little boys would always start calling his name if he was in the front yard. Risky would meet them at the curb, so that they would pet him. People would ride by on their bikes and say, "Hi, Risky." What was I—chopped liver?

Risky sometimes got me into more trouble on the canal bank. We were walking one day, and a man and his dog were walking toward us, the dog pulling at the leash and wanting to get at Risky. Because it was on the canal bank, I almost never had Risky on a leash. The guy yelled at me and asked if I was going to leash my dog. I told him Risky was fine and was no threat. After the man repeated his demand, while his dog was pulling and growling, I told him that I was not the one who couldn't control his dog. He didn't like that, but we just kept on walking. I am pretty sure his dog would have reacted the same way if Risky was leashed.

A couple of weeks later we were headed up on the canal from the south end when we met the same guy.

He yelled again and said, "There is the guy who thinks he owns the canal bank and doesn't leash his dog." I then reminded him that there was not a leash law on the canal but that both of us were trespassing. He walked up to me and bumped my chest, with his dog lunging at Risky. Risky just ignored the dog and kept walking, so I decided to do the same, stepping around the man and his dog. I never saw the man or his dog after that. I did remind Risky that it was his fault I got into trouble.

Except for the main road through the neighborhood most of the streets did not have sidewalks, so we basically had to walk next to the curb on our walks. The speed limit was twenty miles per hour, but the majority of people drove anywhere from forty to fifty miles per hour. We had a few close calls from people driving high speeds and not watching the road. If I hadn't hit the break on the leash one day, Risky would have been sent flying through the air. I tried many times to get the police department to come out to slow these people down, but they did not have the manpower or the time to sit in subdivisions to write a couple of tickets. What happened to protect and serve?

I'm pretty sure Risky put his mark on every mailbox

post in the neighborhood, some two or three times. I kept his leash on during those walks through the subdivision. Many a dog would bark or growl at him and then go through the smelling procedure; if they lingered too long, he would snap at them to let them know he had had enough.

One day we were on Caribbean Street when a garage door opened up and two dogs came straight for Risky. The owner was yelling for them to stop, but when the first one, a pit bull mix, got a little too close, and Risky quickly put him on his back. Risky was pretty mild mannered, but he could also take care of himself. The guy asked me what kind of dog Risky was; he was surprised he took down his pit bull mix.

Grand Junction only averages about seven inches of rain a year, so it's too costly to water the yard with city water. Most subdivisions have homeowners associations to take care of the irrigation water. Big pumps got water to the different filings, which was their main responsibility. The city had miles and miles of canals to service the population. They pulled water out of the Colorado River to fill their ponds, so irrigation water was readily available to those who needed it. Risky loved the canal, and as you have already discovered, he didn't like to swim. He had spots along the canal where he could get in, get a drink, cool off, and then shake dirty water all over me. The sides of the canal had pretty steep slopes, but Risky would get in up to the bottom of his belly and walk along in the canal for twenty or thirty feet before getting out. I never could figure out how he could walk on the slopes and look like he was standing up straight. I assume he was paddling with the outside leg, but he never told me how he did it. As he got older, I taught Risky how to traverse to help him get out of the canal.

In the winter when the canals were empty, he liked to run back and forth, crossing over or just walking down in the canal, finding something to smell. There were times when, if he crossed over to the other side, he would take off and run across a busy road. There was some traffic on the road, but he never seemed to notice. A couple of times I lost him on the other side, and it was too steep for me to try to cross, so I had to call Tonya at work and have her drive down the blacktop to look for him. She always found him though. Another time I lost him in a field full of rabbit brush. He was in there playing chase with another coyote. I circled around the field and headed back up the canal bank. I saw a lady on the other side and asked her if she had seen a funny-looking black and white dog. She pointed down the canal bank and said he was up at the top of the hill, and it looked like he was looking for someone. We were so glad to find each other.

Tonya took Risky to the coal mine with her a lot. There were a lot of varmints for him to chase and maybe even catch. They would see ground squirrels, rabbits, prairie dogs, deer, and on occasion a bear; once they even saw a badger. He had to have stitches in his leg one time when he cut it going through a barbwire fence, chasing a rabbit. One day Tonya was talking to Brant, who owned a fruit stand on the property, when Risky took off straight up the mountainside after deer. Brant remarked that that was the fastest dog he had ever seen.

Another time Tonya was at the mine and a contractor was there in a bulldozer, working on a coal refuse pile. All of a sudden Risky took off up the side of a hill, where two large coyotes were. Tonya called for him, but he just kept going. Tonya called me to help look for him, so I headed out to the mine that was about twenty minutes away. Just as I pulled off the interstate, Tonya called and said the contractor told her Risky had come back to his pickup, so he gave him some water and let him in the truck. I drove up as Tonya was walking back to the truck, and we decided that maybe she shouldn't bring him there anymore because of the coyotes. I said, "Well, we could do that, but he loves to run, and if coyotes trapped him, at least he would be doing what he loves best." I went back home, and Tonya took him to the fruit stand so he could get some water and some attention from the employees there.

Let's talk about snakes. Risky was afraid of all snakes. He would get close to them, but if they wiggled, he jumped back. We saw several big bull snakes, but he usually went out of his way to stay away. We saw a lot of garden snakes on the canal, and he would get brave enough to mess with a snake the size of a pencil. He still jumped back at the slightest movement though. One day he actually picked up one of the little ones, but when the snake wiggled, he would tossed it in the air.

Risky
2005-2019

SIX

When we met other people on our walks, Risky instinctively knew if they were dog people or not. He would go right up to people and stand close to them, so they could pet him and scratch his ears. We sometimes ran into our friends Jim and Debbie on the canal, and she usually had a treat for him. Risky always tried to stick his nose in the pocket that had the treats. There was another guy who gave him treats when he saw him and even walked by our house occasionally to give him treats. Risky also had our UPS driver, Doug, trained to give him a treat when he came down our street. If Doug saw him out in the front yard, he would come down the street to give Risky a treat, even if he didn't have a stop. Risky was always waiting for him at the end of the driveway. If we were walking in the neighborhood and Doug saw Risky, he would bring the dog a treat. When summer rolled around and Risky got older, he would not even get out of the shade when UPS showed up, but Doug would still go to him with the treat. Risky was so spoiled.

We got the oil changed on the car one day and went inside to wait for the service to be done. Risky usually made the rounds of those waiting, to see if he could get a back scratch. He was on the leash and as I was paying for the service, when I heard someone laughing behind me. I turned to look behind me, and Risky had backed up between a man's legs and was getting a back scratch. I apologized, but he told me it was fine. Risky loved having his back scratched and would stand there all day.

I liked to lie on the floor sometimes, and Risky would come to me and sit down on my hip or side, and a couple of times, he sat on my head. He loved to pose for pictures, and one with him sitting on my head was priceless. I have arthritis in my neck, and sometimes on walks I would have to stop and lay down on my back, my head on the ground. Risky would, of course, come sit down on me. A lady driving by one day stopped to see if I was okay, and I replied that I was fine except for this dog sitting on me, but he would let me up in a minute. She laughed and drove off.

Risky was a pest at times but also very loyal and very smart. I am a diabetic and also deal with getting lightheaded or dizzy at times. I always carried hard candy with me, in case my blood sugar got low. One morning we were headed west, down Summerhill Drive, when I got really wobbly and had to stop and bend over for several seconds. As I straightened up, I felt a nose on my pocket where the candy was. I reached in my pocket and popped a candy in my mouth. He stood there next to me, trying to help hold me up, and after a few minutes I was ready to go. As much as he stopped to sniff or went ahead or behind me, he was always watching out for me—best dog ever!

Sometimes for our walk we would cross H Road to a different subdivision. Jim and Debbie lived there. One time when they were out of town, we were watching their house for them. We stopped in to check on things, and I called Tonya to tell her Risky and I would check everything out. About a month after that, we were over there one day when it was raining. When we got to the driveway, Risky headed toward the house and around to the back door, where we had gone in the time before. I told him I didn't think Debbie was home, and he looked at me and then ran around to the front door. I rang the doorbell, and Debbie answered the door and gave Risky a treat.

A few years after that, Jim and Debbie moved into a neighborhood just north of us, where we walked in the field. New houses were being built, so we tried to stay out of the way, but if Risky saw a contractor outside, he was curious to see what they were doing. I would remind him that he didn't know anything about how to build a house. We kept going down the street, and when he got to Jim and Debbie's new house, he turned and went up the driveway. He found Jim inside, watching contractors install the HVAC system. I wondered how in the world Risky knew that they had moved.

Risky loved cold weather but didn't care at all for going anywhere when it was hot. In western Colorado we could have a lot of hot days in the summer, even reaching triple digits. Generally I would walk Risky as dawn was breaking in the morning, and Tonya would wait until around 7:00 p.m. to take him out. We kept him trimmed short in the summer to keep him as cool as we could.

Winter was Risky's favorite time of year. We got more snow than usual from about 2012 to 2016, and he loved to go outside and lay in the snow and sleep, sometimes for hours at a time. One day, after a couple of days of snow, there was about eight inches of snow in the backyard. I gave him a treat and watched him as he went around to the north side of the house. He started digging in the snow, dropped the treat in the hole, and covered it up with his nose. He ran around to the east side of the house and, with tail wagging, he dug up a treat. I don't know how long it had been there; I guess he was rotating stock. Our neighbor looked outside one day and saw Risky covered in snow, so she went out to check on him. He looked at her as if to say, "I'm good." In the fall, when the leaves were falling, he would get completely covered with leaves.

I took him to Canyon View Park one day, so he could

run in the snow, another thing he liked to do. After about thirty minutes, we headed back to the car to go home. He was in front of me, and he turned around and lay down in the snow. He gave me that look, as if to say, "I bet you can't see me."

I just laughed and said, "Risky boy, I see you."

The workers at the park had made tire tracks in the snow from their carts. Risky looked over at one set of tracks, got up, and laid down in a track, as if to say, "Now you can't see me." Risky was one funny dog.

04/01/2012

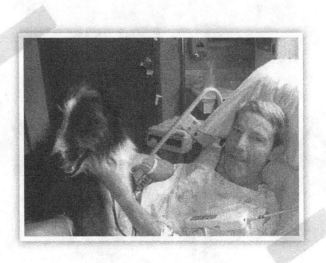

Risky
2005-2019

SEVEN

We moved into our house in Paradise Hills subdivision on Labor Day weekend in 1986. We had five pickups, a two-ton flatbed truck, and a forty-foot trailer. We moved everything but the swing set in one trip—the only way to move. The wives of the guys helping us stayed around a few hours to help Tonya get everything put away, and to thank them, we hosted a BBQ the next day. That tradition continued for over twenty years, and as the kids got older, the crowd grew from twenty to forty, with kegs full of beer and beer pong. I even did a keg stand one day, at sixty years old. At that point we reduced the size of the parties by cutting down on the number of kids invited.

We still had a few BBQs after that, but they were much more tame. We had had Risky a few years when our daughter Kasey gave us a granddaughter, Aiyana. At one party my son and a couple of friends decided to play fetch with Risky, but they quickly found out that when Risky had the ball, they weren't getting it back. No matter how hard they tried, it was Risky's ball. Aiyana was about eighteen months old, and after the boys got tired, I told Aiyana to go get Risky's ball and throw it for him. Every time the boys got close, Risky had the ball and was all the way across the yard. But when Aiyana walked over, he let her pick up the ball and throw it. She couldn't throw it very far, but from that day on, Risky would only let Aiyana throw any of his footballs or stuffed animals. They became good buddies that day. Risky would let her lay down with him on his bed, and he would roll over on his back so she could scratch his belly. She loved giving him treats, and they generally made a game out of it. Those two were made for each other.

Risky
2005-2019

EIGHT

Let's visit Risky's eating habits. He would not eat popcorn, and I had never seen a dog that didn't like popcorn. I think he once saw Hawkeye Pierce on *M*A*S*H* smell his food before eating it because he would do the same thing. If he didn't like the smell, he would not touch it. Sometimes I had to change brands of dry dog food because he would decide he didn't like it anymore. He even got to the point where he would spit it out on the floor or in his water bowl. I would mix soft dog food with the dry, and he would eat around the dry or spit it out. Even if I mixed some kind of meat with it, he completely stopped eating the dry version.

On occasion I would make a vegetable beef stew and mix some with his food because at least he would eat most of it then, except for the corn. There would always be twenty pieces of corn and a couple of carrots left in the bowl. He evidently didn't like corn of any style. He loved lasagna or spaghetti and would clean his bowl every time he ate that. When we grilled steaks, I had to buy New York bone-in steaks, so he could have the bone. He had to be quick because Tonya also liked to gnaw on the bones.

Risky had a water bowl next to his food bowl, another out back, and one out front, but his favorite was the bathroom bowl—if you know what I mean.

We took Risky up on the Grand Mesa a couple of times. The Grand Mesa is the largest flattop mountain in the United States. There were lots of trails up there and plenty of things to smell. We never took him off the leash, though, because we were afraid he would take off after something. More importantly, it was the law to use a leash there. We walked and explored some and let him drink out of a few of the many lakes. I am pretty sure that was one of his favorite places to go.

On a trip to Denver to see our kids, we took a little detour to see friends in Monument, Colorado, and took Risky with us. Richard and Tina Durham had a two-story house on a hill, with a great view of Pikes Peak. Risky had started having trouble with his back legs, so we limited him to the downstairs where our bedroom was. There were plenty of rabbits and several fox that came around pretty often, and although he would look hungrily at them, it seemed he didn't really want to chase anything at all.

Risky went other places he wasn't supposed to go. Valynn came by one day to pick Risky up and loaded him in the back of her truck with her dogs. Risky wasn't used to riding in the bed of a truck. They headed to Safeway to pick something up for dinner.

Valynn went into the store. While in the store, she heard someone say that there was a black and white funny-looking dog in the produce section. When she told us what had happened, I was kind of doubtful because we knew he did not like corn or carrots. But sure enough, it was Risky, and she got him back to the truck and in the cab.

I took Risky to Lowes once to buy tools, but he had zero interest. One day I went to Big O to buy new shoes for the car, and he got to bug a lot of people in the waiting area before I took him outside for a little stroll. One lady was particularly annoyed for some reason, but we were out the door before she could tell us why.

Risky
2005-2019

NINE

On our walks through the neighborhood, we would often see a rabbit, prairie dog, or cat. A few times, when a rabbit would run across the path in front of him, Risky would start to take a step in the direction of the rabbit before he remembered he did not want to chase anything. He would quickly look away, as if he hadn't even seen it. Early in the morning, before our walks, he would go out back to take care of business but stop at the end of the deck and bark a couple of times. I think Risky was telling the animals to go hide, so he wouldn't have to chase them. One morning we were walking down our street, and I saw a cat sprawled out asleep on the hood of a Volkswagen. I said, "Risky, look at that kitty cat." I knew he saw the cat, but suddenly Risky looked the other way. As we walked by the car, Risky never even took a peek at that darn cat. Besides, that cat would have scratched his eyes out.

Risky had many places to sleep other than my spot on the bed. He had dog beds out on the deck, in the garage next to my toolbox, and at the foot of our bed. His favorite place was in the living room, directly in front of Tonya's spot on the couch that had a recliner attached. I'm not sure how many times she had to tell him to move, so he would go to the other end of the couch and lay down on the floor, his back to us. It didn't take much for him to lay down with his back to us. He did it if he did not get a treat, we did not scratch his back, or for a number of other reasons we could not understand. At times he would come in from out back and go all the way across the room, never looking at me, even if I called him. If he did look my way, it was a pretty dirty look. When he did get up and come over to me, he would put his head against the front of my recliner because he wanted his head and ears scratched. Once he got tired of standing there, he would go lay back down, again with his back to me.

I retired two years after we got Risky, so we spent a lot of time together. We got to where we understood each other and communicated pretty well. On our walks through the neighborhood, I could tell him to turn left at a certain street, and he would, or I could tell him to turn on Del Mar, and he would. Sometimes I would even decide on the next turn and see if he would understand, and many times he actually did. Maybe it was just blind luck that he went that direction—who knows? Sometimes when we left the house he would stop at the end of the driveway and look several times toward the park on his left or to the west down our street. Occasionally I had to make up his mind for him.

Later on, after he had slowed down a little and stopped chasing anything, the long daily walks barely made two miles, but they were done in the same amount of time. The older Risky got, the slower he got. I started calling him "Molasses," along with other names I had called him through the years. I called him "Dig Dig" the first time he dug a hole in the yard. When he hurt his leg trying to dig prairie dogs out of their hole, it was "Sir Limps a Lot," and when we were in the desert, I called him "Mr. Risk." Sometimes I even called him "Dawg," but when I did, Aiyana would sternly remind me that his name was Risky. She would say, "How do you expect him to come when you call him 'Dawg,' Pop Pop?"

One day we were out in the yard, and I was blowing leaves out in the street. Risky was all the way across the lawn, trying to sleep. My blower had stopped, and I was talking mean to it, so it would run again. I finally finished and looked around for Risky, and he was nowhere to be found. I got in the car and went up the street toward the canal bank, and I saw him turn the corner to the path that led to the canal. I parked and went after him, and when I got on the canal, I yelled at Risky and asked him where he thought he was going. Risky just looked at me and took off headed north, so I followed along. About forty-five minutes later we made it back to the car.

Risky would hide in the bedroom if anyone yelled while watching a football game. And if I was ever on the phone with the cable company, he would go stand in front of the back door and I would let him out. Risky did not like loud!

We had a sliding back door to the backyard, so every time he wanted in or out, I had to get up. And even though the sliding door to the garage was only six feet from the front door, sometimes he could not decide which door he wanted to go out. One day both doors were open, and he just stood there staring at me. I didn't know dogs could get Alzheimer's.

Even as Risky got older, he could still get me in trouble. We were at the park one day, walking around the pond, and Risky was about sixty feet away, marking his territory and fences that backed up to the park. A couple was walking toward me with a dog that was pulling at the leash. As I met them I said, "How y'all doing today?"

The man said, "Not very good because your dog is not on a leash."

I then pointed out that he was thirteen years old, sixty feet away from their dog, and minding his own business. By then Risky was ahead of me and still along the fence line. I kept going, and for the next two or three minutes, the man was still yelling at me and calling me names. Can't we all just get along?

Risky
2005-2019

TEN

We would drive to Palisade sometimes, about nine miles to the west of where we lived. There was a park that ran by the Colorado River, and it was one of Risky's favorite places to go. We parked pretty close to a spot that had a ramp to put boats in the river. Risky would head straight to the ramp and down in the river. It wasn't very deep in that spot, so he would stay in the river for several minutes. When he finally would get out, we would head west along a path just a few feet from the river. Like the canals, he had certain spots where he could get in the river to cool off. At times the river was pretty high, but he was always looking for a place where he could see the bottom.

The park was a good place to walk Risky, and we usually ran into a lot of people walking their dogs. We would see some of the same dogs a lot, and Risky would get a lot of exercise when chasing and playing with them. We generally spent a couple of hours there on the different trails and any other place he wanted to smell.

We often ran into a lady friend I had known for years, and we would walk and visit while the pups did their thing. Her dog was a little smaller than Risky, so of course Risky thought he could knock her dog down. You could tell he enjoyed doing it.

Risky
2005-2019

ELEVEN

Risky loved kids. He really enjoyed Halloween because he always went to the door when the kids came. I was not positive if it was their costumes or because they were just kids. I think it was probably all about the kids; there is just something about kids and dogs that speaks for itself.

I think dogs are one of the best gifts God has given us. Dogs give comfort, love, encouragement, and pleasure. They reduce stress, anxiety, and depression; ease loneliness; help with exercise and playfulness; and even help improve your cardiovascular health. They can also help you to remember to take your meds or a candy to improve low blood sugar. Caring for an animal can help children grow up more secure and active and teach responsibility.

Dogs have been guide dogs, served in the military, and sniffed out bombs. They are great at using their noses to find lost children. Dogs are more than just pets. Dogs can cause the normal brain to produce oxytocin, a hormone often referred to as the "cuddle chemical." From pets to sporting companions to service dogs, canines add a measurable degree of quality to a person's life.

Walking your dog is about more than potty breaks. It provides stimulation, physical exercise, chances for socialization, and opportunities for behavioral training. It gives you and "Rover" a chance to bond and grow.

I have always felt that if anyone decides to pick a dog for their family, they must treat the dog like family. When I see dogs chained up or even in small dog runs, I feel that the owners aren't getting the joy and love from "Spot" and everyone is losing out. Dogs love unconditionally and forget quickly. They seldom hold a grudge, and it doesn't take them long to get over it. You would be amazed at how well dogs can communicate, if we just listen. Risky and I talked a lot; my wife thought I was crazy, but that was okay with me.

Will Rogers famously said, "If there are no dogs in heaven, I don't want to go there." I have to agree with him. But if God can get Noah to load a boat with all the animals two by two, God can surely find a place for dogs in heaven.

Risky
2005-2019

TWELVE

In the spring of 2019, Risky started slowing down quite a bit. He had lost almost forty pounds since 2016 and was looking very tired. Every now and then he would take off and run a short distance or go out the back door and run to the north end of the yard. I could get him to play sometimes, but it was not with the energy he used to have. I would throw his football, and he wouldn't even care.

Richard and Tina came by on their way to California to spend a couple of nights with us in the summer. When we ate dinner, Risky was usually over by me because he knew he could get a few handouts. His front feet had started moving like he was dancing, and evidently that was his new and improved way of begging. It was pretty funny to watch, and it also helped to fill his belly.

A few weeks later I took Risky to the vet because he was still losing weight. She decided to do some blood work on him to see if anything would give us the cause for the weight loss. The results showed that Risky's kidneys were failing. It just so happened that I had been in renal failure for over six years, so maybe he got it from me.

We put Risky on a diet of food less invasive on his kidneys and prayed for the best—and boy, did I pray. I had been telling Risky for months that he had to hang in there with me until he was fifteen. After the diagnosis, I borrowed a line from the series *Longmire*, when Walt told the horse burned in the barn fire that he didn't have to do this anymore and it was time. I began telling Risky the same thing.

Our walks were confined to a walk over to the park and around the irrigation pond. It was only about two-thirds of a mile and took about twenty minutes. You could tell Risky didn't want to go but knew it made me happy. After about ten days of the kidney dog food, he stopped eating it. I called the vet, and she asked if he was still going for walks; I said only somedays. She told me to give him anything he wanted to eat and let him do what he wanted. A couple of days later I walked out with the leash and asked Risky if he wanted to go. We made it only halfway down the street before he stopped, so I took him back. I continued my walks, and he would stand up and watch me until I got out of site. About fifteen minutes later I would turn on my street, and he was looking and wagging his tail. I figured in the twelve years we had Risky, he had probably gone twenty-five thousand miles. We averaged almost 1,100 miles a years, and Tonya and Risky had walked about 900 miles. Risky may have added three or four thousand miles just in the back yard. But watching me leave and return from my walks had become the new normal.

About a week later Risky stopped eating altogether, so I called the vet, and she told me it was time to let him go. I made an appointment for 2:00 p.m. and hung up. After I stopped crying, more like sobbing, I called Tonya and told her. I'd had triple hernia surgery a few days before and wasn't to pick up anything over fifteen pounds, so Tonya said she would be home to help.

I went outside and lay down with Risky and started talking to him. I didn't have to tell him a thing—he knew. He knew it was time. You could see in his eyes that he was tired. Tonya got home a little after one o'clock and took a few minutes in the yard with Risky. We left a few minutes later, headed to the vet, and I wanted to turn around two or three times and take him home, but having to do what was best for Risky would be best for us.

We took Risky inside, and they escorted us to a room in the back, where we could be with Risky. He was standing up when the vet gave him the sedative that would take fifteen minutes. He fought it the whole way before finally laying down. I laid down eye to eye and told Risky how much I loved him and that I would never forget him. Risky whimpered for just a second, so I told him again that I loved him, and he made the same sound again. I knew it was okay. The vet gave Risky the shot, and we looked into each other's eyes for the last time.

We had to put Hobbs down years ago, and I was too chicken to go in with him, which is something I always regretted. Your face should always be the last thing a dog sees.

It has been two months since we lost Risky, and I still lose it every now and then. Risky would have been fourteen in December, and we had him three days shy of twelve years. I have put several more pictures of Risky on the walls. My wife went to Texas a couple of weeks ago, and she told me before she left that if there was wallpaper of Risky all over the house, she would kill me. I'm still breathing.

Risky
2005-2019

THIRTEEN

Our kids came home for Christmas in 2019. We loved having them home during the holidays. I had decided to have some shirts and hoodies made for presents. I had a T-shirt made for me and Aiyana and a hoodie for Tonya. On the front was a picture of Aiyana and Risky, and the back had a large picture of Risky's face. As we were opening presents, Aiyana opened her shirt and immediately started to cry. So did I. Tonya said, "Thanks for making everyone cry."

Even though I say over and over that Risky was the best

dog ever, I know a lot of people could say they have the best dog ever. We all have our own reasons as it relates to our best friend, and I am pretty sure they are all very true. One of the things about Risky that in my opinion made him the best dog ever was his sense of humor. As I have stated, he loved to play tricks on me every chance he got.

One day when our granddaughter was here, she was helping me wash windows, which mostly consisted of spraying me with the hose. Risky was watching closely, hoping he wouldn't get sprayed. I had sprayed him a few times in the summer, just to cool him off. He really didn't like it and always ran away out of range. He was watching close when Aiyana was spraying me. He would come over to the hose and step on the sprayer but couldn't get it to work. It was pretty funny watching him, until he hit the sprayer just right and it was a direct hit right in the face. Aiyana was laughing so hard as Risky turned and ran into the neighbor's yard—yeah, he got me again. I picked up the hose and pointed it at Risky but sprayed my granddaughter instead. I was pretty wet but decided it was worth it to see him try to spray me back. That was the last time I sprayed him. I love that boy.

Risky Business—best dog ever

CPSIA information can be obtained
at www.ICGtesting.com
Printed in the USA
LVHW051343281020
669933LV00007B/482